LIFE IS A SONG

in the key of love

or Growing Up with the
Embarrassment of Prejudice

By: Helen Marie Szollosy

in
ε of it
ALL !!
Make
fe a
Song of It

Helen M. Szollosy
11/2015

LIFE IS A SONG
By
Helen M. Szollosy

Self published by the author: www.lulu.com

ISBN 978-0-578-00690-1

Library of Congress Control Number: 2009901580

Dedicated to:

the 'little black boy' walking past my house, in the alley, in 1964, who was such a strong, innocent spirit as to want to venture out of his neighborhood to explore the world, only to encounter confusing, angry, shouting from the adults around me to "GO BACK TO YOUR OWN NEIGHBORHOOD"! He was the inspiration for me to write this book.

Also, to Cheryl, Khantalay, and Warnel; who shared their stories, educated me, and asked that I write this book.

Encarta dictionary definitions

Prej –u-dice (noun)
1. Opinion formed beforehand. A preformed opinion; usually unfavorable based on insufficient knowledge, irrational feelings or inaccurate stereotypes.
2. Holding of ill-formed opinions based on insufficient knowledge.
3. Irrational dislike of somebody – unfounded hatred, fear, mistrust of person or group. Especially one of a particular religion, ethnicity, nationality, sexual preference, or social status.

Ster-e-o-type (noun)
1. Oversimplified conception: an oversimplified, standardized image of a person or group.

La-bel (noun)
1. Descriptive word or phrase: a word or phrase used to describe a person or group.
2. Brand: a brand name of some items of fashion.

   Personal note: *...to place a mark or brand on someone. False label = uninformed label.*

AUTHOR'S NOTE: Any word, terms, 'labels' used in this book are not meant to offend, but to relay personal experiences. Racial, ethnic, religious or sexual terms are used as they were experienced by me at the time the experiences are being recalled. They are used to emphasize and teach how a child or adult may be impacted by hearing or experiencing these terms.

I would like to express my wish for the acknowledgement of the worth, and value of all living things, without prior judgment, no matter how they are outwardly expressing in this lifetime.

LIFE IS A SONG

Lyric by: Joe Young; Music by: Fred E. Albert

Don't be afraid of the future
All of our plans will come thru -
How can they fail, with love on our side,
They'll never fail, we won't be denied.
All the world's a symphony
For you - and me.

Life is a Song - Let's sing it together - -
Let's take our hearts - and dip them in rhyme -
Let's learn the words - Let's learn the music - together -
Hoping the song - lasts for a long, long time ...

Life is a song, that goes on forever
Love's old refrain, can never go wrong
Let's strike the note, Mendolsohn wrote -
concerning Spring weather -
Let's sing it together

AND MAKE LIFE A SONG!

Table of Contents

INTRODUCTION

Years ago, I had an idea to write a book about "Growing Up, With the Embarrassment of Prejudice". I came from a family of good, hard working parents. It seemed, in the 60's - when I popped into this world (1959) - people lost site of the 'human race' and focused too much on not liking each other's differences.

The book was to be about me coming into the world, befriending:

- a neighbor boy (close to my age) who was Croatian

- a little 'black' boy who dared to come down to Front St from 5th and 6th street, in Steelton (the 'Black folks' lived on 5th and 6th Streets, the 'white folks' lived on 1st, 2nd and 3rd Streets. It was 'understood, that we didn't cross these lines. I didn't know why?

- a girl who came from a very troubled family that was shunned - where they were known as the 'So and Sos) - *as if their last name was the description of a 'race' or 'culture'.* I found out, as I got older, that the family name used to describe 'the people we didn't want to associate with' was actually a dysfunctional family who had an alcoholic, abusive father. This resulted in the family being broken up. I also found out later, that my mother would give hand-me-down clothes to the nuns at our church/school to give to the family, anonymously. I need to share this to balance the prejudicial remarks I may share to show that prejudice isn't always realized – and can come from basically 'good' people – due to lack of awareness and education.

I wanted to write about the confusion I felt as a 4-5 year old, standing at the gate at the end of our duplex-yard - looking out into the alley - as my neighbors would yell - "We're going to call the cops!" when the 'Blacks' of the 5th and 6th street homes threatened to come down into the 1st and 2nd street homes (white populated). The confusion I felt when I was told I could no longer play with the little Croatian boy, next door, due to family feuds.

I remember standing there, at the end of the yard, inside the gate, with an adult or older sibling standing beside me, looking out into the alley, at a potential play mate, darker skinned, with a runny nose, who just happened to decide to go out and 'explore' (unknowingly crossing the racial boundaries of Steelton), and thinking - 'OK, tell me again, WHY I'm not supposed to like 'this' or 'that' person...???' WHY can't I play with the little 'black boy' that walked past my gate at the end of the yard? WHY can't I play with the girl who seems really fun and friendly but is known as coming from 'The So and Sos'?

I wanted to write about how PREJUDICE is TAUGHT and LEARNED and spreads like WILDFIRE, when people give into their egos and detach from their inner spirit. Not recognizing the soul within vs. the outer appearances and culture/race/religion.

I never got the book off the ground because I didn't want to seem as if I was whining or judging my family. I come from good, hard-working parents who I saw - many times - totally give of themselves - unselfishly. I saw my dad's best friend from his Bethlehem Steel working days was a 'black man' named Willie. I saw my mom, go to stay and visit with neighbors who were dying, when no one else wanted to be there. Yet, I also saw them 'automatically' talk in ways that were prejudice - because it was a LEARNED trait - due to bad, past experiences by their background or culture.

Prejudice evolves from a personal life experience that gets blown out of proportion. It evolves from a culture, race, individual in charge, tribe, etc. who - as the result of that personal experience - bleeds their feelings into others. For example -

A key person in a tribe has a fearful experience, meeting someone from another race. Out of that fear, they run back to their tribe and announce how - 'this thing that happened to them as a result of the different person they didn't understand' tell them that - they should not like nor accept this other 'race/culture/religion'.

Prejudice comes out of someone or some group feeling fearful or wronged, or not understanding another person, group or way.

Prejudice is beaten by removing that fear, lack of understanding and forgiving a wrong; most importantly, sharing that discovery with those that have been infected by the disbelief that caused the prejudice to mutate.

As Reverend Jim Rosemergy says, 'We are one race, human.'

Here's to enlightening ourselves and the world!
High-lighted-Helen (living **bold** and in *italics*!)

We experience,

We create,

We Teach, and

We Share

Prejudice and Intolerance.

We have the power to:

Overcome the experience,

Relook at the experience,

Educate ourselves, and

Share what we've learned

about overcoming

prejudice and intolerance

to

MAKE LIFE A SONG!

By: Helen Marie Szollosy

CHAPTER 1

RECOGNIZING THE MONOTONE

"GO HOME!" "GET BACK TO YOUR NEIGHBORHOOD!" "I'M GOING TO CALL THE COPS!" These are the words I was hearing as I saw a potential playmate wondering down the alley, at the end of my yard. The words were coming from the mother of the family living in the duplex house attached to ours.

There I was, 1964, standing amidst the adults as they yelled at this little boy. I didn't know why, I was just 'learning'. As a 5 year old, I was being educated by the adults around me, to not accept the little, dark skinned boy. I didn't, yet, know why. These adults would be educating me.

Like me, the little boy wasn't afraid to leave his house, his street, his neighborhood to explore. I had done so, on my own, being a free spirit. I was known to wonder the alley, go up to 2nd street from Front Street, to show off something as magnificent as my vaccination shot! This little boy was just like me, or so I thought. The adults around me were teaching me differently.

I stood there, looking out at the little boy, listening to the yelling, looking up at the adults, trying to take it all in. I have such a clear memory. The little boy was snotty nosed, a little unkempt, a little ashy-skinned around the face. He was just walking like there was no problem. I know I didn't see the problem. But, being the silly kids that we were, what did we know? All we knew, was that we had been born into this fascinating world worth exploring and sharing, and that's what we intended to do, until we found out otherwise.

So, from that day on, he realized he was to be considered different and less than, and I was not to consider associating with this little boy, because we came from different neighborhoods. Lesson not understood, but lesson noted.

I've been waiting 44 years to write this book, and it bothers me to have to relay this incident. Even at the age of 5, I knew it didn't feel right. I think there is a real reason I held on to that visual and auditory memory. I feel I was meant to recall it at the right time in my life, in order to share it.

The prejudice being taught to me just didn't relate to skin color. Being outgoing and loving to explore the neighborhood and meet other kids, I brought home a playmate one evening. There I was, in the back yard, having fun with my new girlfriend, slightly older than me, but having fun, nonetheless. When an older brother arrived, the little girl was screamed at to leave the yard! The little girl didn't know what was wrong, but listened to my brother. I cried and cried, because my new friend had been taken away from me. The girl was referred to (years later I realized it was just her last name) as a 'so and so'. (I'm purposely excluding the family name to honor their privacy.) I was told 'not to play with or invite any of those '*so and sos*' into the yard, ever again'! I was confused. I didn't know what a 'so and so' was? I thought it was a reference to another culture. I ran into the house crying to my mom.

Oh, the reason I thought the 'so and sos' was a reference to another culture label is that I had been told not to play with the little Croatian boy next door.

Evidently, we weren't supposed to like the Croatians.
We were Hungarian. So, when I was told not to play
with the 'so and sos', I thought their last name was the
name of another culture. Fascinating how kids interpret
things. That's another story in itself.

So, by age 5, I was being educated: 1) don't allow the
dark skinned people into our neighborhood and don't
play with their kids, 2) Don't play with the 'so and sos'
(members of a certain Caucasian family who lived by
lower standards); and 3) Don't play with the neighbor
boy, my age, because he is Croatian and we are
Hungarian.

My, all the lessons I had to learn at such an early age!
They made no sense to me, but who was I to question
the adults around me?

Now I'm going to really confuse you. I had an Aunt
that was Croatian! My dad's best friend at the Steel
Mill was a 'black' man named Willie. The Hungarians
and Croatians teamed together when they were fighting
'the blacks'. Well, if I could see how absurd all this
was, as a 5 year old, I'm sure you can.

Here's another irony. My own family was dealing
with: Alcoholism; a mentally/physically disabled sister
as the result of being hit by a drunk driver in 1968;
neglect and incest as a result of all the overwhelming
stress caused by the challenges my family was facing.
This caused a younger sister and me to openly be seen
as 'uncared for' – unwashed hair, unkempt clothes,
missing school, etc. Due to the overwhelming situation
my parents were facing. So, basically, WE became the

'so and sos'. I know my classmates didn't know how to act around me. I came from 'that family with the sister hit by the drunk driver.' I went a whole school year with a torn school uniform, hiding the tear (held together by a safety pin I had found) by wearing a sweater in the hot weather, because I didn't want to burden my mom with fixing it. I'm sure the body odor was horrendous. My mom was overwhelmed with my disabled sister, 6 other kids, etc. I know I attended school with a rarely washed school uniform, oily, unkempt hair, and was certainly considered a 'so and so' by my classmates.

My father went to work every day, my mother got the meals on the table, paid our school tuition, took care of her elderly mother as well as my disabled sister, etc.

I admire my parents greatly! But, a person can only take so much, and my family was handed a large, trash dumpster loads of challenges! There's no blame here, I'm just making the point that anyone's life status can change.

I'm pointing out how the best, good-hearted, hard-working people can be unknowingly prejudice just by having heard and observed the behavior before, and not being aware the pattern is continuing.

No matter what came out of my parent's mouths, they would have helped anyone in need at any time, no matter who they were. They were selfless, giving, kind people.

It was like we were all being taught to 'role play' prejudice and intolerance, even if we didn't truly feel it or believe it. It was just an 'acceptable' way of behaving. I think that's why I felt comfortable asking 'why', and making my own decisions on how I wanted to treat people, later in life.

The feelings of intolerance and prejudice weren't my parent's, weren't my siblings', weren't my neighbors' or mine; they were learned and inherited from previous generations.

I needed to write this book to show how our actions and behavior leave an impression on children and other adults. I actually grew up to be a very tolerant, accepting individual, but somewhat confused by the words and comments I would hear from the adults around me. The actions and words were contradictory, to what I could see as beautiful souls, inside.

I was asked to speak at a local club whose purpose it is to "…change the world, one child at a time." It's a wonderful group of business people who network as well as pull their resources to donate time and money to help children.

The talk I decided to give is titled, "Careful, the children are listening'. I feel it is so important to watch how we talk and act around children. As I've shared, from the start of this book, the actions of the adults around me, when I was around 4 to 5 years old, left a big impression on me. What I'm grateful about, is that I realized I should question the behavior.

So, let me get into my discussion on looking at intolerance and prejudice and comparing it to music.

Did you ever think of how boring the world would be if there was only one type of, externally expressing being or type?

- one outer appearance
- one type of sea creature
- one type of bird
- one type of cloud
- one season
- one hair color
- one skin tone or outer shell
- one vocal tone
- one height

a monotone world, boring.   *snore....*

Yet, *because* of all the differences and diversity, we have 'issues'.

Can you imagine what it would be like if we couldn't place certain sheet music markings or notes next to each other because "they didn't get along"? The sound, quality and variety of our music would be very limited.

For example, "Uh, sir, you can't place that whole note next to that half note! It's just not done! They'll NEVER get along, and besides, they don't have the same length and value, they're totally different!"

Another example, "Uh, m'am, you can't place that rest symbol next to that series of notes – that's a lazy rest symbol, it's going to have a negative impact on those fast moving notes!"

Or, you could just hear one type of musical note talking about itself: 'Hey, I'm a brief sounding staccato note, I think we should all be brief and fast!" With the longer held whole note arguing, "We don't want your fast note types on this sheet music; we only want long held whole notes!"

Sounds silly? Well, sounds like ignorance, which breeds labeling and prejudice, if you ask me.

Even if you aren't familiar with music, trust me, not allowing the logical order and flow of writing music to occur, would create some very sour notes, some real prejudice on the song sheet.

In my own, ever-evolving, process and search to become a better person, I realized that we need to look at our lives, and the world with 'new eyes'.

I believe we need to play the tape back and start from the beginning of our entrance into this lifetime, and ask, 'did what I see and feel really happen as what I thought and felt?' What?

Are my views and assumptions based on truth, or on my personal perception as a child, or on the personal perception of an adult/mentor that was 'stamped' onto my conscious/sub-conscious? Not necessarily with the intention to cause harm, but coming, sometimes, from wanting to protect those from the unknown – culture, etc. It's all about fear.

Now that I'm an adult, capable of making my own decisions and conclusions:

o   How do I truly feel about a particular race,
    culture, religion?
o   Do I want to educate myself more and find out
    the facts of a particular race or culture,
    religion or spiritual belief?
o   Did a particular situation in my life really
    happen the way I saw it, or were my
    conclusions based on the views of an
    uneducated child, dealing with fear and
    confusion, or an adult's impact on me as a
    child?

I'm asking you to relook at your life, step back, walk
around the events and experiences, and look at them
from different angles, from a new view/perception, as
an educated, open-minded human being. Do they look
any different when you see them from 'different views',
or as an educated adult?

This is something that will take a while to do. You
might want to write down your views on different
personality types, cultures, races, religions, etc. Make
note of each feeling and ask yourself: Where and when
did I develop this conclusion? Is it one that I wish to
change? Many of us don't even realize we hold a
prejudice or label until someone makes us aware.

This may make you to want to go to a particular person,
group, etc., and talk to them about your feelings, letting
them know that you now draw new conclusions. This
can be very healing for both, you, and the person,
culture, religion, group, etc. It is forgiveness in action,
on both your parts. It's very freeing.

I'm told we teach what we need to learn. My honesty with myself forces me, on a day to day basis, to look at my personal feelings about people and situations.

I do a regular self-check with myself to see if my behavior is coming from a false, embedded prejudice, label, stereotype which I feel. I do this, because it impacts my effectiveness and success in this world. If I make false assumptions, and don't approach people or tackle a challenge because of a false prejudice, it holds me back from experiencing life.

For example, I started a laughter wellness group at which a wonderful variety of people attended. There were young, old, different physical ability people in attendance. One of the older members, who was also in a wheelchair, and has a slight slur to her speech, would appear to finish one of the laughter exercises a little later than everyone else. It worked out to our advantage, because it prolonged the healthy laughter. Well, here's where my own presumption/prejudice came into place. I thought this person was older, disoriented and just not able to keep up with the rest. I learned a very strong lesson. I openly talk with the attendees at my laughter wellness class, sharing freely. I talked directly to the older woman in the wheel chair, at the next club meeting. I found out, that she felt the laughter exercises we were doing needed a 'big finish'. This is why she would always appear to be lagging behind.

Well, I apologized right then and there! I acknowledged her expertise in choreographing the laughter exercise, apologized for making an assumption that she 'just wasn't able to keep up', and since then, we have incorporated her suggestions into the club!

Being the wonderful soul that she is, she forgave me and shared how she felt what I was doing was so wonderful! I'm blessed she, as an 'Older, Wiser, Forgiving' woman, was so kind in helping me to learn a lesson. I discovered I had a prejudice and was making a false assumption about her abilities as a senior person.

Whenever I hold a laughter club, I make mention of her and her contributions.

One of the things I started to do on a regular basis, to learn more about people, is to ask people I meet from different backgrounds and cultures, how to say: Hello, Good-bye, How Are You and Thank you, in many languages. This opens up a rapport between me and others. I am then able to educate myself by learning directly from people. I keep in mind, that the person I'm talking to is one view, not representing an entire race or culture or belief.

I usually have to share information about my own culture and beliefs in order to get others to share. But, I feel it's worth it in the end. It usually ends in a smile due to sharing and accepting one another. Okay, to be honest, sometimes it doesn't.

For example, being an outgoing person and enjoying meeting people of all backgrounds and cultures, I readily open up and ask questions, to learn. This has gotten me into trouble on several occasions.

When I held a decorator/sales position at a furniture store in the early 1990s, I encountered a gentleman with an unusual accent. I asked where he was from. Well, didn't I open a can of worms, the response I received was, "That's just like you Americans, none of you know your geography!"

What did geography have to do with it? I just wanted to learn more and didn't recognize his accent. Turned out he was Lebanese, but spent so much time yelling at me, for asking, that I never learned anything about his country, first hand. Did that cause me to hate everyone from Lebanon? No. Do I think everyone from his country is like him? No. Maybe he was having a bad day? I don't know.

Here is another example, while holding that same job in the early 1990s.

Did I let the above incident keep me from moving on? No.

There were a couple young, handsome furniture delivery guys setting up some furniture in one of the store display windows. The company had sent them to set up a large item in one of the display windows.

So, once again, I recognized an accent and asked where they were from? The one gentleman answered, Israel. I was excited! I had never met anyone from Israel! I asked what it was really like to live there, because we only ever hear about it on the news, which always shares the negative.

Well, even though he was a little annoyed, he said –
"It's not like that at all, your news only reports the bad
stuff." I thanked him for sharing this information with
me.

I have a good friend, Cathy, who is an African
American. What I loved about Cathy was that she
acknowledged my 'ignorance' regarding certain phrases
I used and their meanings. Cathy was such a good
friend, she would gently say, after I had made a
comment, 'Do you know the meaning of that phrase
and its origin?" I would say,

'No', and she would let me know it was something that
was 'off-color'. I was always so grateful that Cathy
accepted me, my intelligence, my worth, and felt
comfortable enough with me to gently educate me.

As an adult, Cathy moved to Florida with her husband,
they had children. Being an intelligent woman, Cathy
easily found a job. When she was pregnant with her
first child, she was fired from her job due to prejudice.
She had to temporarily get a low wage, part-time job
due to her pregnancy. I accidentally got in touch with
her when she came back to visit her family in
Pennsylvania. She shared with me how shocked and
disappointed she was with the coworkers that didn't
stand up for her when she filed her complaint. She felt
utter disappointment for these coworkers who were
from the North and she felt, shouldn't have had feelings
of prejudice against her. As I'm writing this, I'm
realizing the sick feeling of knowing the prejudice we
still feel between the North and South and how we
'lower and raise' our expectations of how Northern and
Southern residents should feel about varying skin tones.

It's amazing to think that still exists, today. Hence, writing this book.

Just because we 'learn prejudice' doesn't mean we have to hold on to it as adults. Befriend someone whom you feel prejudice or unease towards, let them know you want to learn more about them, first hand, not from 'other people's assumptions. Educate yourself! *Education and release of fear about the unknown is what overpowers prejudice.*

When I was walking into a grocery store the other day, I heard a father say to his two children, as he walked behind me: **"Now THAT'S an example of exactly why we can't tolerate those people!"** I felt so much pain over the comment. His children had just been introduced to a prejudice based on his personal view and experience.

It's so important, when communicating, to note: 'this is MY personal perception based on MY personal experience, which I am choosing to heal.' It's human to feel hurt, pain, confusion, fear - it's human to develop conclusions based on those hurts, pains, confusions, and fears. It's BEYOND human, spiritually healing, to know that you can evolve and heal past those feelings to see the GIFTS in all our experiences!

CHAPTER 2

IT'S GOT A GOOD BEAT, BUT I JUST CAN'T DANCE TO IT or *STOP PRESSING THE REPLAY BUTTON*

Just think of all the ways in which we can be prejudice. As I've said, I'm constantly recognizing my prejudices, laughing at them, becoming more aware of them, feeling shock, and seeing where I want to take a different view!

- Religion
- Culture
- Hair type/texture
- Sex
- Career
- Lifestyle
- Type of car driven
- Race
- Hair Color
- Lack of hair
- Voice/accent
- Vocation
- Age
- Social status
- Type of foods one eats, and so many more...

Have you ever thought or heard yourself say, I just can't understand or relate to _____?

It's OK to not be able to RELATE to whomever or whatever. It's your human nature. It's normal to be CAUTIOUS, it's a survival mechanism. Be aware and forgive yourself. Take time to realize why you feel as you do. It's OK to let a person know you have trouble relating to them. Embrace the differences. It's OK to 'ask for your space' due to feeling uncomfortable about 'them' or their culture, etc. Open communication coming from a place of love and respect is a good thing. Make sure you do this 'one on one' and not to impress a group of peers. This is personal.

It's NOT OK to cause harm, hate, or make life difficult for 'them' because of your personal perceptions and feelings. It's NOT OK to 'bring people on the bandwagon' with your fearful feelings in order to justify your fears or discomfort. **THIS is PREJUDICE in its most sorrowful form**.

In this chapter, I want to share a series of encounters I've had with people of different backgrounds, cultures, races who asked me to make sure and write this book, due to particular situations that occurred in their lives, as a result of prejudice and stereotyping.

I think it's important to site actual occurrences over the last 20+ years to prove my point that prejudice is still alive and well, among us.

I had doubts about writing this book, but then I would read an article or hear of an occurrence that pushed me forward in writing this book. Here are examples of personal occurrences and new articles from the last 20 years:

1960s

I asked a senior member of my family 'why' my ancestors didn't get along with or like another culture that was constantly discussed. This other culture was known as: 'those loud, rough folks from an area known as little Chicago.'

This person said it had something to do with people from that culture in Europe, taking fruit and vegetables from the farms of other cultures during WW1 – rather than providing for themselves, asking etc.

I just stood there when I heard the response. Again, the person I asked is one of the most intelligent, giving, sacrificing souls you'd ever want to meet. I asked a question, and she gave me an honest answer.

Evidently, a 'story' or 'label' had started across the natives of a particular country due to the 'bad behavior' of some people from another culture. This label then got placed on the entire culture!

This bled over into the next generation, after WWII and over into America, with the families that migrated. The hate festered and got to my generation, where I would see my neighbors fight with my family because of the different cultural backgrounds, with finger pointing etc. It's amazing.

The other amazing part is that our cultures would band together when fighting the African Americans living in the slums, three streets north of our homes!

Again, I repeat, I would stand at the end of my yard, listening to these adults yelling at each other, teaming with each other and making absolutely no sense to me whatsoever, even if I asked "Why"? I wasn't more than 5 years old.

I honestly think I was meant to write this book from the day I was born. I always felt like I was looking out through eyes of: None of this makes sense to me!?

Growing up in the 60's in South Central Pennsylvania, we felt the effects of the equal rights.

The area in which I lived was segregated. Walking home from school could cause racial tension as well as cultural tension. Our Catholic schools/churches were also divided between Slovenian-Hungarian, Croatian and Italian backgrounds. On the one hand, they were separate to allow for the priests to say the mass in the native language, so that isn't necessarily a bad reason. We even had to be let out of our classes earlier from one of the other ethnic schools, due to possible fighting between the two schools/churches. I used to ask myself, and we're all Catholic, aren't we supposed to Love One Another? This was a very confusing message for me as a child and young adult.

As younger generations attended these schools and churches, not having the language barriers, it no longer made sense to keep them separate.

In 1995, while the horrid fighting was going on in the Baltic States of Europe, the local Catholic Church diocese decided to blend the ethnically-separated churches into one. Several Steelton, PA churches were combined into one, known as Prince of Peace, Roman Catholic Church.

This caused grieving for the older Croatians of the area, who had had this church as their own, since it was built. They had embraced, loved and nurtured this Catholic Church and School.

The new church name was significant in bringing the ethnically-separated churches together; Prince of Peace.

I remember one church member telling me that, at the first service, a man was standing outside on the sidewalk, handing out pamphlets to 'fight the consolidation.' The wonderful thing I was told is that the parishioners IGNORED HIM! This is what we need to do, NOT give power to prejudice!

All the parishioners were Catholic, it didn't matter that they were from different backgrounds. Steelton had finally grown and evolved. It was a wonderful expression of how segregation and prejudice can be overcome!

Back to the 1960s –

I remember one of my older sisters telling me a story about some 'black' (African-American) girls chasing her home after school. She dropped a pen during the chase. She told me when she stopped to pick up the pen, the girls stopped. When she picked it up and started to run, so did the girls. She relayed the story to me as if to say "we are only playing our roles, a game, and there is nothing to be afraid of. This removed my fear and allowed me to be more relaxed.

My sister later became a teacher.

As I said earlier, knowledge and education are the keys to releasing prejudice. What we relay and teach to those around us, can INFECT a society and make it feel at ease. We can spread peace and acceptance or disease. My sister could have taught me to be angry and fear the girls that had chased her; instead she relayed a positive story.

I can tell you I heard many racial or ethnic slurs in my household, no matter how 'good' my family was. It was an *unaware* behavior.

As a child, in learning mode, I picked up words and phrases, not realizing their derogatory meanings, or that they could cause a person to feel hurt.

This is why my friend Cathy's gentle education, became so important to me, while working with her in the 1980s. She was always so nice as to let me know, what I was saying and how to correct it, without being angry with me.

What we share with our siblings and children about experiences…. How we portray them and SEE them – can make a MAJOR change in a lifelong chain of events…It can instill prejudice and fear – or change a person's entire outlook.

SO IMPORTANT!

Television's Impact – 1960s

What I found really wonderful, was how the television show, Star Trek, taught the absurdity of prejudice. This show brought to mind different life forms interacting with each other.

One particular episode, I remember very clearly, because it blatantly showed the absurdity of prejudice. The Star Trek Enterprise crew encountered a world that consisted of beings whose facial coloration was a mirror image, causing prejudice.

One half of the population had faces that were black with white polka dots on one side of the face, and white with black polka dots on the other and vice versa.

Captain Kirk was trying to reason with the people on this planet to stop fighting just because of their facial differences. He talked to both sides. During the show, the side with one look accused the side with the other look of being more aggressive and uncultured, or something like that. They had 'labeled' the one group of people.

Captain Kirk had to make them realize that their assumptions, labels and lack of knowledge of the true nature of the 'other' members of their race caused their constant turmoil.

I always felt it was so wonderful that this television show of the 1960s *DARED 'TO BOLDLY GO, WHERE NO SHOW HAD GONE BEFORE'!*

1970s – Star Wars

Think about the movie, Star Wars, when it was introduced. Think of the characters entering one of the 'inter-planetary' bars or clubs. There is a scene where Hans Solo, a main character, walks among all the beings of the other planets, 'hanging out at the bar'. It was such a wonderful scene to watch. Forget about 'White', 'Black' (Caucasian, African-American), Asian, Native American, Male, Female, etc. – this went to a whole other realm of acceptance! Television and movies can teach great lessons.

1980s

When I was working at a full time job in the 1980s, we had, what I can only say I truly don't understand, a cross burning occur on the lawn of a Black family who had moved to the West Shore of Harrisburg. It was very disturbing. While my friend Cathy and I were walking to our cars in the parking lot, she shared how scared she was as a result of hearing about the cross burning.

This was the 1980s! This was my friend Cathy – not my black friend Cathy, just my friend Cathy. I don't think I had any response, at the time. I know I had very deep feelings, mainly of possible anger, confusion, frustration, knowing that, I would do anything to help her, if needed. I was disgusted that a human being would think of doing anything to cause such fear in others' lives. I didn't know what to say, all I could do was listen.

She continued that she was more concerned due to cars openly displaying the confederate flag license plate. In my ignorance, I asked why. She noted it was an open symbol of racial hate.

There I was walking with my friend, not knowing what to say. There were times, when I had offered to 'speak for her'. But, Cathy always felt it was best to 'let them be' – due to their ignorance and not wanting to cause further problems. This really bothered me, yet I also admired my friend for her sensibility, intelligence, understanding and forgiveness. I was often very humbled by Cathy.

Early 1990s

Being an open, friendly person, a lot of neighborhood
kids would stop by my home, visit with my pets, sit on
my porch swing, etc. I got to know their parents, too. I
lived in a wonderful, mixed neighborhood when I
bought my first home.

I had wonderful Greek neighbors, living across the
street, who were so helpful! I had wonderful Irish
neighbors to my right, who were like angels to me,
helping with my yard work. I had Asian neighbors,
African-American neighbors, etc. I loved the
neighborhood.

One day, I visited a senior member of my family and
told her how my friendly Afghan hound had caused a
little girl in the neighborhood to giggle and giggle,
because my dog loved her so much and was licking her
all over the face!

The family member responded, "I don't know Helen,
maybe you don't want your dog to get too familiar with
'black' people in the event you are ever robbed."

Knowing this person was an intelligent, kind, good,
hard-working soul who would help anyone in need, I
knew she didn't really mean what she was saying.

I said (feeling shocked by the whole statement) "White
people are robbers, too." She snapped out of it and
agreed.   I'm sharing this to show how one bad incident
can mar a person's thinking. My family had been
robbed by an African-American man, when I was about

10 years old. He had staked out our house, come in the early morning hours, propped open all our house doors, and then stole my father's entire paycheck. One family member had awakened, due to being sickened by the 'substance' he had sprayed through a window fan to make people sleep. The man worked at a factory and had access to chemicals.

If this family member hadn't gotten nauseous and awakened, the robber wouldn't have been discovered. Our family dog knocked the man's paycheck out of his back pocket while he was trying to run out of the house. The police then knew who he was.

I share this to let you see how one, negative incident can cause prejudice to sneak into the mind of the most good-hearted souls. This is why I do constant self-checks on myself.

I saw how that affected this person, even being the selfless, giving person she is. Emotional events can cause momentary prejudice.

Late 1990s

Kevin is a young man I worked with at a summer job in the late 1970s (an African-American). Oddly, years later, I bumped into him when I went to have lunch at a local Mexican restaurant. We were in separate booths, dining alone. I recognized him and called him over. We shared stories about our summer job fun and caught up on where we had been etc.

I told him about my idea to write a book about 'Growing-Up with the Embarrassment of Prejudice'. He said "Write It!" He then proceeded to tell me about having gone to school for theatre, dance, the arts. He mentioned he had gotten a job in one of the New England states. He told me about a particularly disturbing experience he had while riding the bus. He noted that he had gotten on the bus and sat down. An older woman got out of her seat, came up to where he was sitting, stood in front of him, and just started yelling racial remarks at him.

If you ever met Kevin, he is the most clean cut, preppy-looking young man you've ever want to see. He is very gentle and soft spoken. He had been raised to be respectful of women and senior citizens. He said he just sat there, stunned. He didn't want to cause the woman harm, but didn't know how much of the verbal bashing he should take. The woman got off the bus before him.

He said, what bothered him most, was that not one other person on the bus had gotten up and come to his defense. Not one person had stood up and asked the woman to Stop!

He asked me to make sure I write this book.

The year 2004 –

I dabbled in on-line dating/matching sites for a few years. I agreed to meet a man from a northern, rural area outside the city where I lived. I had good friends from this area and was familiar with it. So, even though it was a distance from where I lived, I agreed to meet him for dinner.   The first date was fine. He was a very independent business owner, intelligent, and preferred to dress casually. I appreciated that he was his own person.

When I agreed to go on a second date with him to a restaurant located in his town, I saw a totally different side to this man. I actually became fearful. While sitting at the restaurant in his small, mountain town, he let me know how he would never want 'alternate lifestyle' (he used other descriptions) people brought to his home, if we continued to date. He expressed that, he wouldn't want African Americans (again, other words) in his home, etc. I had told him, and reminded him, that I was actively involved in theatre and the arts. I told him, and reminded him, that I had friends of different lifestyles and racial, cultural backgrounds. I noted that these were my friends and I could never harm them by even sharing what he was expressing.

I was sitting at a restaurant, out in the open, fearful of what he was publicly stating. I suddenly felt, 'am I sitting with the head of the KKK here?' (Yes, my fear had caused me to put a label on him.) His hate was so open! He expressed his disgust with African Americans because of a group of teenage/African American boys, who had come into their town and urinated on the outside of one of their town buildings.

Which brings me to my earlier discussion; do we label an entire race because of what 3 teenage boys did? No.

I shared this with him. He basically stated, 'we' don't need those 'kinds' of people here.   I just sat there, wondering if I was going to arrive home safely.

He also shared his distaste in upper class Caucasian residents who had moved down the road from his rural business.

I was very glad when dinner ended; I got to my car and let him know that 'I didn't think it was going to work out' to say the least!

This was the year 2004, and I saw and felt such prejudice and hate in this person, it caused me to be fearful.

I had friends not too far from his town that were beautiful, accepting souls. I was educated and aware enough to know that his views weren't shared by everyone in his town.

The year 2006 –

I took a television of mine to a local second-hand television and electronics store. I had the television for many years, it had died, and I bought a new one. I wanted to make sure it got disposed of properly. I took it to a man who calls himself "Chief". Sadly, the reason he calls himself that is because he is from India. He did that because he said, many Americans thought he was 'American Indian' not from India – and he got that nickname. I told him that was sad, so he started to share a story….

He said, when he first came to America, he moved to the West Shore of Harrisburg. [This was a predominantly white community – known (not so nicely) as the 'White Shore' in opposition to the East Shore of the Susquehanna river, which was the inner-city of Harrisburg, PA]. He said his only intention was to work hard and provide for his family. He shared that when they got their place to live – there was a knock on their door within the first few days.

He said some people from the neighborhood came to his home – not in a friendly manner. He said they sat in his home and explained that if he did anything to bring their neighborhood down, or cause any problems, they would make sure to have him removed.

This was a wise man, like my friend Cathy – I am in total amazement. He could see the ridiculousness of what was going on. He didn't argue; he just assured these people that he had the best of intentions, and would make sure to keep himself in check. I thought this was amazing.

He said, years later, these people are now his good friends. He recognized that they didn't know anything about him, and that they were afraid.

So, this is a somewhat happy ending, noting that by using understanding, recognizing their fear, and lack of knowledge about him and his culture, etc he was able to give them time to get to know him.

He also shared with me, that he had lost a son, years back. I felt very privileged that he trusted me enough to share his story with me.

By the way, I had donated my television to him to give to a needy family. He replaced a burnt out part and passed the television on. What a special individual. It is for him, also – that I write this book.

The year 2007 –

I enjoy Thai food. I got to know a couple local families from Thailand and Laos. *When I was talking to one of the daughters who attended a local college, I shared my idea about this book.*

She said, Oh! Please write that book! You don't know how bad it was when we first moved here! We lived in the city of Harrisburg and were treated like we were stupid, just because we didn't speak the language! (American English) I really felt for her. She is a very special acquaintance/friend of mine, now. She is so giving, intelligent, hard working etc. She graduated from college, was active in international relations at the school, participates in missionary activities through her church etc. Once again, I would stand up for her if I ever heard she was being harmed.

Hence, for this beautiful soul, also – I share her story and honor her by writing this book.

August 2008 – Shenandoah Beating/killing of Mexican (Pennsylvania Newspaper Article)

Another vigil for unity planned in Shenandoah
by the Associated Press
Wednesday, August 6, 2008 7:09am

SHENANDOAH - - A second vigil calling for racial unity is being planned in the small Pennsylvania coal town where a Mexican immigrant was beaten to death.

The pastor at the First United Methodist Church is planning a Reconnecting Healing Service for 3 pm Sunday.

The Rev. Bruni Martinez says the service is to bring the people of Shenandoah together after Luis Eduardo Ramirez Zavala, 25, died July 14, two days after being beaten.

Three teenagers were charged in the death of the farmhand and factory worker.

What happened in the above, so recent, incident? I understand alcohol may have been involved, other than that, I don't know the details. My personal perception would be lack of education in relation to two different cultures. Fear about lifestyles and cultures as well as communication gaps, prejudice playing itself out to a very sad ending. A sad ending not just for the soul who lost his life, but also for those still living who have to 'live' with their actions, wondering - What in the world happened? I don't honestly feel the persons involved in the above story intended for anyone to be killed.

The wonderful thing that came out of it was the Hispanic minister holding the candlelight vigil. There's something good in everything. Awareness is so necessary, acknowledgement. Otherwise, healing can't take place.

When I shared my feelings about the above article with family and friends, I received the following feedback.

What follows are the comments of a mother of two, showing her concerns about prejudice and intolerance in relation to raising her children:

... "thinking we were beyond this type of behavior"

... When we were living in ... (1980s), I was appalled at the prejudice there. It was white vs. black, Union vs. Confederate, Yankee vs. Rebel, and the South shall rise again! Just a little microcosm in the whole human element, but the shock waves in that part of the country have lasting effects. ... has the highest per capita murder rate in the country...and it is black on black, due to the frustrations and the never-ending suppression of their culture. I was glad to get out of there...I was not sure what we would do when the kids got to school age because we could not afford a private education and the public education was sub-standard. The private education would have made them bigots and the public schools would have gotten them shot.

A friend shares their recollections on growing up in this area back in the 1960s:

This was and is really sad.....this is up in the coal region not so far from where I grew up... when I was growing up..maybe in elementary school there was a young girl who was bi-racial... some boys splashed gasoline on her and tried to set her on fire.......she was lucky as only part of her legs were burned..... I

remember growing up with only white people around
me........

Laramie, Wyoming beating/killing of a homosexual
man
[Play: *The Laramie Project, by Moises Kaufman and*
Members of Tectonic Theater Project]

My familiarity with the above occurrence came from
watching a stage play about the tragedy. I was uneasy
about going to see the show, but was thrilled at how the
facts were shared as well as all the positive actions that
came as a result. The play revolves around all the
wonderful events that occurred in the town, after the
homosexual man was found beaten. We don't always
understand WHY something happens, but to see the
positive results among people bonding, working
together, after something like this happens, honors the
person whose life was taken.

The play showed how the town came together,
expressed their feelings about the incident, and many of
the positive results – not having 'Matthew' die in vain,
but to have had purpose to his short life.

One of my favorite quotes is one I came across while
attending High School in the mid 1970s. This quote is
also placed on a plaque at the City of Harrisburg's
Peace Garden, along the Susquehanna River.

"ALL THAT IS NECESSARY FOR THE FORCES OF
EVIL TO WIN IN THE WORLD, IS FOR ENOUGH
GOOD MEN TO DO NOTHING." Edmund Burke

When a hateful crime of prejudice or intolerance occurs, one of the best things we can do is to band together and make the statement: THESE ARE NOT MY BELIEFS AND I WON'T ACKNOWLEDGE THAT HATE WITHIN ME! Then, without hate, without prejudice, bless and pray for the souls involved. Fighting hate with hate is a losing battle.

I need to share, that at the time of writing this book, many positive changes have happened in the area where I live!

I now live on the formerly known 'White Shore.' I am out and about a lot, and I can honestly say I see a wonderful change occurring.

I see people of different cultures, races, religious beliefs, etc intermingling with one another, in a healthy positive manner. This brings me joy!

So, why am I writing this book? I see some of this same behavior still occurring here as well as in countries around the world. I'm hoping that by writing this book, we each become more aware as well as make the rest of the world aware!

My goal is to not have history repeat and repeat and repeat itself.

As my mother told me, when I shared that I was writing this book; 'it NEEDS to be put in writing, Helen.'

So now let me take you into the next chapter; comparing intolerance and prejudice to working itself out on a sheet of music. If it can be worked out in the beautiful sounds of music, it can be worked out in the beautiful expression of our souls.

CHAPTER 3

LET'S GET DOWN, GET FUNKY – *CREATING A NEW SOUND*

So, how do we start to fix this? How about looking at the diversity of creation, life, like a song, on a sheet of paper?

Don't worry if you've never looked at a sheet of music. I'm going to break it down bit by bit and explain how 'LIFE IS A SONG'. I'm going to explain how we can beat our own personal prejudices and global prejudices by seeing Life As A Song, With New Eyes!

Let's start at the beginning:

<u>G-CLEF</u>

If you look at a sheet of music, there's this strange looking, squiggly thing that looks like this:

Its purpose is to anchor or hold it all together. Non-spiritually, think of the "G"-clef as the GLUE, GOODNESS or GROUNDED. Spiritually, think of it as 'GOD', or your higher power of choice. It's just how we each choose to look at it.

Without the 'G'-Clef, everything would fall apart!

The center swirl/point of the G-Clef points to the line denoting the musical note 'G'. It's like saying – let's get grounded before we take a walk across the sheet music. G-Clef is a 'Good' place to start!

STAFF

Behind the G-Clef are 5 lines known as the 'STAFF'

Without the STAFF, we would lose our variety; we would have MONOTONE, one note.

[Think about sitting at a piano, playing one note over and over and over.... makes you want to scream, doesn't it! **Stop the Music!**]

The staff may represent different levels in society:

- o   levels of financial status,
- o   levels of thinking,
- o   heights in physical stature, or
- o   Countries.

It also represents *separation* - lines vs. spaces, isn't that interesting? It's all in how you choose to look at it. Holding things together **OR** keeping them separated. *That's something for discussion!*

BOTH the lines AND spaces are needed; otherwise, we would have one solid-line-bar with no variation of higher and lower notes. i.e., a middle C vs. a high C in music theory

For example: In society, if everyone was poor and just stayed in that state of living vs. aspiring to something greater. Relating to music, it would be one note played on one line, over and over. No variety.

Isn't variety the spice of life!

KEY SIGNATURE – a key signature determines which scale is used to write the music. A couple examples are the keys of C and G. In mid-eastern music, the music has a different quality/tone because the musical scales start on different notes than our Western Culture. It's what makes the music so unique! Isn't that wonderful! I learned this by going to a mid-eastern music concert at my local college.

It seems the parallel with us would be voice differences or lack of a voice, i.e. the deaf community. Do accents, speech impediments, higher and lower pitched voices make you think differently about anyone?   Do you think differently about a man with a higher voice or a woman with a lower voice?

I have to be honest, with my low voice, over the telephone; I've been called 'Sir'. When I let the caller know I'm a woman, there are always apologies. I just laugh and say, no problem, it works for me – I have a torch singing voice with a unique quality! That gets the person on the other end talking to me, and getting to know me other than by the 'sound of my voice' alone.

So, I find 'this' interesting. It shows how a unique quality which could cause someone to judge me, also allows people the chance to start talking to me and getting to know me. More and more, I'm seeing how our 'differences', when ALLOWED to be discussed, can work to our advantage as a society, in helping us to communicate and educate ourselves.

A friendly question about a 'difference' allows for open communication. A comment made out of hate or fear, closes any immediate chance for communication or education.

On a sheet of music, you may note different symbols directly next to notes (sharps (#), flats and naturals). These are used to bypass the current 'key' or scale (which impacts the sound).

In life, there are times when:

A person may need to march to the beat of a different drummer.

A person may be 'a little different' because of:

Brain Damage	Alcoholism	Fear
Emotional Abuse	Learning Disability	Mental illness
Physical Impairment	Physical Disability	

They may have been 'previously' accepted by society, but now they are shunned or treated differently (labeled or stereotyped) because of one of the above, or some other reason. They go off the beaten path of 'the norm', but they are still a member of the human race. They still need love. They still have a purpose in the Song of Life.

Speaking of labels ...

My oldest sister was hit by a drunk driver in an auto accident when she was 19 years old (1968). She is now 61 years old. My sister graduated 13th in her High School graduation class of 500 students. She graduated with honors and got a job with the State Department in Washington, DC.

She decided to return home to attend college, and then become a foreign correspondent. Her plans were cut short on a rainy/snowy day in March, driving my 2 yr old sister down a road to pick up a brother from his music lesson.

Upon impact, she flew head-first out her locked, passenger-side car door. She was in a coma for 3 months and it is a miracle she is alive. The blessing is she has her intelligence, the curse is, she has front, upper left lobe brain damage. She had to learn to speak and walk all over again.

The reason I bring this up? Whenever anyone meets my sister, it's instantly thought that she is mentally retarded, and she is talked down to. This is due to the interesting sound of her vocalizations, when in fact, she is highly intelligent, with a slight speech impediment, and partially paralyzed on her right side.

Whenever I am with her and someone approaches that doesn't know her, I feel the need to introduce her as:

"This is my older sister, Dolly, she is highly intelligent, but brain damaged as the result of being hit by a drunk driver."   As a protective, younger sister, I want to shield her from being talked down to.

Another reason I am writing this book.

TEMPORARY CHANGES TO NOTES

I had an interesting experience at lunch today; that fits into this section. I encountered, from myself, temporary labeling or assumptions when talking with the manager of a restaurant.

She's a lovely soul, from Scotland, married to a French-Canadian. I noticed an accent when I first met her. She smiled, because she said she tried so hard to hide her accent. Why? I asked. She said people couldn't understand her when she spoke her native accent.

Well, today, when I ran into her at lunch, her voice was soft, low and throaty. I asked if she had a cold. She responded no. I said, 'because it sounds like a very seductive voice!' I had to stop myself in mid-sentence because I've gotten myself in trouble, before.

I have a theatre background, and I find accents and voice tones, qualities fascinating! It's like studying dialects, accents, tones, qualities, styles, when I'm out and about, meeting people. So, at times, I come across as intrusive or offensive when I comment on a person's voice, conversation style, etc.

Here's where education comes into play. In talking with this manager, I found out that TEMPORARILY, every morning, she has this 'style voice'. She said it was the result of having to take medication. I asked if the medication dries out her vocal chords. She explained, 'No, it's because it makes her nauseous, and she gets sick.' I then realized it was more serious.

She continued, 'I have a brain tumor that is non-life threatening, which is monitored by doctors, but I have to take medication so as to not have seizures at night.'

Well! I asked her if I could share our conversation in my book. I had only ever talked to her in the afternoon, so I just ASSUMED she had a cold, or something. Then, I went on to make comments about 'how her voice sounded, seductive, sultry, etc. Can you imagine how a TEMPORARY change in a person's daily life, such as she experienced, could make people jump to conclusions, especially if this was happening to a child in school.

We can all experience TEMPORARY times of being in the MINORITY.

Another example I personally experience was while attending school in Pittsburgh, PA and staying at the Duquesne dormitories. I was heading back to my room one evening, got off the elevator, and was surrounded by a huge, heavily attended dorm party. It just so happened, the party was attended by all African-Americans. Did this bother me? No. Did I suddenly realize, 'you know, is this how an African-American or some other minority feels'?

I attended a church and school and lived in a neighborhood with all white (Caucasian) children, due to it being ethnically populated with, Hungarian, Slovenians, Croatians, Serbians, etc.

I think, at different times in our life, for example when I worked in a male dominated Information Technology field and office, we feel the pressure of being in the minority.

The reason I stress this, with the above examples is; by seeing how being a minority feels, why would we ever think of making someone in the minority feel worse, less than or unwelcome?

I really think it's all about awareness and being in touch with your feelings. Basically, being aware of the Golden Rule; to treat others the way you would want to be treated.

So, to continue with how this all parallels to music…

Staccato note [brief and to the point] - this type of note is indicated by a dot being placed beneath it. It has its own 'label' to give it its identity.

A couple parallels in relation to life:

- o   a succinct or blunt person, doesn't mince words
- o   a very brief occurrence of an action that can cause a large impact!

vs.

A note that is asked to be __ held, or drawn out; for example, a note at the end of a song.

In life, this could be:

- o   The teenage years
- o   An unexpected delay, i.e. pregnancy
- o   Temporary unemployment

This is a great one for me with which to relate! I'm outgoing and fast paced. It's difficult for me to have to slow down, stop what I'm doing and sit and listen to someone that is slower paced in their speech and movement. I've actually read a book on communicating and relating to different communication styles because of this.

What I'm saying is, we may not relate well to someone that doesn't speak with our style and pace and we may have trouble understanding. The key is to make the effort.

Let's look at the symbol for making a note go SHARP – this takes a note slightly higher than it would normally be in the existing key signature or musical scale.

o Sharp minded
o Cutting tongue personality
o Harsh moment in life
o Intellect (IQ)

A Sharp or Natural symbol can change the key mid-song) –

Some examples of changing temporarily or shifting one's perception would be:

o   Personality, mental capacity, emotional health
o   'Social face', such as low income to higher income, then going bankrupt.

This is an interesting one. For example, a person from a low income area, coming into money – being accepted by higher society, and then not being accepted if losing the money and moving back into the lower income area.

Speaking of Intellect...

A person can hold a specific prejudice about a person whether they are uncomfortable around a highly intellectual persona or a lower intellect person.

I recall my younger sister mentioning, a girl in the neighborhood, at her high school saying something to the effect: 'you're in those smart classes;' hence, not including her in their group. This hurt my younger sister's feelings. She was excluded because of her intelligence.

Interestingly, I hung out with/played with the older sister of the girl that made this comment. Her sister didn't seem to mind that I was in Honors classes. We each had gifts to share. Her sister was more relaxed and OK with herself. I never felt that her sister was lesser than me. She had talents that I didn't have. It didn't matter how we scored on tests.

I scored well, not from studying hard, but just because of the brain and intellect with which I was born. My friend didn't score well on tests, but was a very confident, giving, outgoing person who was accepting of me. She wasn't shy and I was. So, forget about the 'sharp mind or wit' – as with sharps in music, it didn't matter, there was no prejudice there.

<u>FLATS – this takes a note lower than it would normally be in the key signature or scale</u>.

A dull personality	A quiet soul
A boring moment in life	An abused soul

Do we sometimes ignore people who are quiet and don't reach out? Do we tend to stay away from someone who is emotionally scarred or abused due to not understanding them? With these instances, sometimes the only thing we can do is be available to listen. We can't truly understand what the person is going through. Sometimes, it's a matter of listening and letting a person be, till they are ready to open up, rather than forcing them to open up when they aren't ready. Acceptance and tolerance is very important, here.

NATURALS – these bring the note 'back' to the existing 'scale' or 'key signature'.

Some parallels in life, relating to the 'natural' symbol:

- o   'Laid back', easy going personality

- o   Easy going life experiences, no ups or downs

- o   A recovered alcoholic, abusive person, gambler, etc.

Curves or Arcs hold a group of notes together...
- o   a temporary bond to achieve a goal or purpose
- o   i.e. charity drive, gang gathering or unification

This symbol in music bonds other objects. In life, it can be a group coming together for a cause. I see gangs forming out of necessity, due to lack of direction from adults and the need to take control and survive; strength in numbers.   So this can be a good thing or a bad thing, depending on the purpose of the group.

<u>MEASURES</u> – these keep the music 'organized' into segments. These keep 'order'.

This is like society's rules that give people a 'clue' as to how to behave in a given situation. For example: 'traffic lights'.

Measures are defined by a vertical line about every inch on the sheet music.

Without order, the world would be chaos. In life, these rules are defined by society and people choose to follow the rules, to vote for politicians who enact these laws.

How do we feel about people who 'dare to be different', or who dare to step outside the lines, think outside the box, etc?

In music, this can be seen as a 'partial measure' or a 'pick up' measure. It doesn't have the same amount of beats as a 'full measure'.

<u>TIME SIGNATURE</u> - Time signature determines the number of beats per measure.

4/4 Time Signature = 4 beats per measure -
3/4 Time Signature = 3 beats per measure – Waltz etc.

Some examples of how this parallels with life:

- o A hurried/rushed moment in life, a 'fast paced' society vs. a slower paced.
- o A peppy, fun moment in life.
- o A steady, flowing moment in life.
- o Mood swings vs. easy going state of mind
- o A religion or culture with a quieter, low-key approach vs. a
- o Highly expressive, upbeat approach.

None of these are 'wrong', all are a choice. The variety adds to the uniqueness of the music. It's what determines a:

Waltz, from a Rumba, from a Polka, etc.

How often something occurs in life? Is life erratic or steady?

MOOD – the feel of the song.

In relation to life, *'with Feeling'* – (sorry, in advance, for the below 'labels' used as examples…)

- o Loving (sometimes refers to the Italian or French cultures)
- o Staccato – brief, quick occurrences. Once in a lifetime opportunities
- o Boldly – really living life! Olympic wins!
- o Loud – Forte! Having your voice heard!
- o Expressive!   Flowery, colorful speech.

- ○ Soft – pianissimo (quiet moments or people.)
- ○ Meditative (Oriental, Hindu, Buddhism, Mid-Eastern)
- ○ Fast – Efficient people. Get the job done.
- ○ Slow - Depression
- ○ Moderately – moving through life easily

BASE CLEF

Treble or G-Clef

Bass Clef

- ○ Lower income
- ○ Lower mental capacity
- ○ Lower-minded
- ○ Lower moments in life that made us feel beaten, lost...

This is also the steady pulse or beat in life, looking at it from the positive.

Sometimes, when the economy is great and a community is living in harmony, the beat is steady and light.

Other times, in times of chaos and uprising, the beat is intense and hurried.

The background beat of life changes with the flow of life.

<u>CHORDS</u>

Some have a pleasant sound; some have a harsh sound - depending on the mood desired by the composer!

Chords are groups of notes, so in life, they can represent:

Gangs	Associations	Cultures
Clubs	Religions	Deaf Community
Races	Lifestyles	

Whenever I question why I should be writing this book, all I have to do is look at the news. Here are a couple examples:

As recent as 1995, the Lancaster, PA area had a White Supremacist group organize a march. No, the majority of residents in that area did not agree with this, but according to constitutional rights, they had the right to march.

The only way to overcome something like this is to release FEAR and encourage EDUCATION.

I also found more recent comments from former residents of that same area:

July 2007 posting re: York, PA

The courts of York just awarded $45,000 to a white supremacist group that tried to get a permit to have a march in York last year but was denied. They won on a technicality - however, the fact that they are still trying

to organize marches let's you know groups like the
KKK are still very active in York. I will say that each
time they've tried to march - the people of York have
managed to shut them down. They may be active, but
they don't appear to be very powerful. However, I can
just tell that race relations are pretty bad overall, which
is why I've decided to leave York after only living here
for 1 ½ years.

This is why I feel it is necessary to write this book. It is
so important not to allow FEAR to step in! We need to
learn from our past mistakes. I'll talk more about this
under the section on 'Brackets'.

<u>REPEATS</u> also includes <u>CHORUS</u>

This is the symbol on sheet music that basically tells the
musician to 'play it again'. If a phrase in a song is
played over and over and over again, it would get
monotonous. Music is smart, there are other symbols to
'get out of the loop' of the repeat.

Humans don't always know how to 'get out of the
endless loop', we need to support each other,
sometimes, step in and say – OK – let me give you the
signal to 'break out of the loop'.

For example: going to prison again, 12 Step Programs,
etc. Learning a life lesson over again, when one hasn't
gotten it.

Instead of judging someone who has 'gotten stuck in
the *repeat* of a song'; have the courage, get in their face

and say 'Hey! This music is getting old, let's change the arrangement!' For example, family interventions.

Such as if a neighborhood is showing prejudice towards different cultures moving in, make the first move in a positive direction and 'bake a cake and take it to their house!' Get to know them! *Ignorance breeds prejudice, knowledge breeds understanding and acceptance.*

<u>HARMONY</u>

Blending voices –
Soprano   Alto   Tenor   Base

Provides the salt and pepper, the spice!

This can be types of cultures and religions, any varied belief system

A Jewish man I worked with told me once that he loved playing Santa Clause for the local fire department! Another thing he and fellow members of his synagogue did was to volunteer to work for Christian-based-belief staff at local hospitals on the Christian Holidays - especially Christmas! This was a self-less gift they gave so the Christian-belief staff could celebrate their holiday with their families! I think it's called a MITVAH, per a friend of mine.

THAT's what I'm talking about! This brings a smile to my face as I write it.

So who is better in this scenario, the Christian or the Jew? NEITHER! We are all one, we are all equal - we all BLEND - making life beautiful. In the above story, we 'let each other be' and GO BEYOND by supporting each other's beliefs. We give service to our differences. I just love that story!

MELODY - Anchors the song

For example: the common flow of society – without the background noise?   How about the Olympics, as an example, or when a multi-cultural group gets together to fight crime in a city? It's when society is living 'in-tune' with the beautiful sound of life. Now THAT'S a beautiful melody!

TYPES OF NOTES

In order to get my point across in this section, I'll be purposely placing 'labels' on the musical notes, described.

Who do you see as:

  1/16th   smallest, dark, quick, speedy
               the UPS GUY in comedy routines!

This note may also be described as more feminine. But, this may be a false label on my part! This note is one of the fastest you'll see on a sheet of music, it can add a hurried feeling to a song, making it exciting!

An example of how 'shunning' or not tolerating this type of note relates to people and labels/prejudice is with **Gender Bias**:

While working in the Information Systems/Technology field, I received an e-mail from my boss one day noting an article out on the internet: 'women don't do as well in the Information Technology field.'

Isn't it interesting that women were felt to be more suited to working with the 1940s ENIAC Mainframe computer. These are the ENIAC women: Antonelli, Kathleen (Kay) McNulty Mauchly; Bartik, Jean Jennings; Holberton, Frances Snyder (Betty); Meltzer, Marilyn Wescoff ; Spence, Frances Bilas; and Teitelbaum, Ruth Lichterman.

But, this is a whole other topic, 'glass ceilings' in the corporate workplace.

I worked with a woman who had all her Information Technology certifications (this involves schooling, extensive testing, etc.), yet a former supervisor also told her: 'You know, women aren't as able to function as well as men in this field.'

Like my friends Cathy and Kevin in dealing with racial prejudice, my coworker and I opted to not argue with the people making these false assumptions. It appeared there was lack of education and knowledge on both their parts. Sometimes, all you can do is feel sorry for the person, bless them and send them on their way.

1/8th smaller, dark, quick, feminine to give some 'labels'

Although small, this note is quick and can add a lot of energy and fun to a song.

I'm 5' 2" tall, while that isn't overly short in stature, it can cause me to go unnoticed around taller stature people. This note size, shape could also parallel how a 'little person', in society, gets treated by 'average size' humans.

What 'is' average? It's basically what the 'majority' is in a particular situation.

For example: I met a woman in a wheel chair at a local retirement community. She wasn't elderly, just limited in her physical movement with her legs as well as her hands.

I talk to a lot of people when I'm out and about. This woman was in the lobby of the building, but trying to open something, struggling with it. Being careful not to overstep, I said 'Hello' and let her know I was 'available for assistance, but would allow her to ask if she wanted it from me.' She thanked me and offered me the item she was trying to open.

She made a comment about her 'limitations'. I started to tell her about a Star Trek episode relating to a female officer who came from another planet with no gravity.

I told her, when the female/alien officer went on the Star Trek Enterprise space ship, she was 'physically handicapped', and had to use a wheel chair.

But, when she went back to her 'cabin', the gravity was removed and she would gracefully float about her room, because this was NORMAL for her.

:

When a fellow officer joined her in her quarters, he appeared handicapped and clumsily bumped into walls, etc. due to not being used to not having gravity.

I told the woman I had met in the lobby, if this planet was populated by more people with her physical ABILITIES, 'I' would be the one that was handicapped.

She said, thank you for sharing that, I never looked at it that way, before. We smiled and parted ways.

No one is handicapped, there's just a NORM, and AVERAGE, and then – there is what I like to call: The PICASSO's. These are the people, animals, plants that 'have such strong spirits, they DARE to be DIFFERENT!' They don't follow 'the norm'.

1/4th [small, dark, not held as long, quick]

This note can break up a monotonous sound and start to add variety to the music.

A couple examples, to parallel life: non-hearing, or hard of hearing; living in a closed world.

1/2   [open, white, not as big as whole note]

This type of note can be another way to break up or slow down the music from a faster pace.

Some examples to parallel life: someone who is average in stature, open-minded, light-hearted, Caucasian?

whole note
O

Whole note [open, white, elongated, big, held for a longer time]

Personal traits comparison in relation to labeling or prejudice -
   o   Large person in stature or size
   o   An open, outgoing person
   o   Hearing vs. not hearing (interesting?)
   o   Caucasian, albino?

   vs.

   A Situation or thing -
      o   A life situation that is ongoing, continuity - a certain life behavior.

Speaking of size…

Here's where I can share one of my own challenges. When I first got in touch with my food addiction, I attended an Overeaters' Anonymous meeting. Years later, I would laugh at myself about this.

I went to the meeting and sat in between two other people that just happened to be physically large. Now, you have to picture that I was 5' 2" and at least 200lbs, myself. Yet, there I sat, feeling totally awkward, which is normal, and thinking: *"I can't stand being here with these fat people!"*

Yes, you read correctly. Interesting, isn't it?

I think we need to see and accept ourselves, before we can remove our prejudices about others. Sometimes, as it is with bullies, a person will lash out at others rather than deal with their own self-criticisms; i.e. someone who isn't book smart, making fun of the smart kid at school.

I've been labeled as incapable of certain physical activities due to my size. I happen to be an excellent bicyclist. I went bike riding with a family member who was a lot thinner than I am, I out rode her on all the hills, climbing them easily. I have great endurance in bike riding due to my strong legs. Keep in mind I am short and heavy.

My sister had trouble keeping up with me. She eventually commented at how surprised she was with my bike riding ability. It was assumed I wouldn't do well because of my size and stature.

I personally don't like school labels and grades. I admire an expert mechanic the same as I admire a physicist. Each is using their given gifts. They are both using their natural talents. I'm sure the physicist is extremely grateful when he goes to an expert mechanic and the vehicle is working beautifully. Yet, in the school system, the Physicist would be placed in an honors/academic program and the mechanic may be labeled in the lower end of the grading spectrum in the 'vocational-technical' end. I feel we should be recognized for the gifts with which we are born, and not whether we can do well on a scholastic test. I did well in school with very little effort; doesn't that say something about the system?

I talk earlier about the separation caused between friends when children are placed in higher scholastic classifications.

Another example would be when I was a mother's helper in Pittsburgh, in the late 1970s. On one of the play dates between the daughters of two families I had to resolve an upset.

It turned out the one 8 year old went off to cry and hide in the garage. When I went to find and talk to her, I found out she was upset because she couldn't do gymnastics as well as her friend.

Her friend, the girl for whom I was responsible, was thin and agile, she was built for gymnastics. The girl that was upset and hiding was short and chubby (built more like me). The short and chubby girl had a beautiful, tone perfect singing voice and wonderful rhythm. She could dance beautifully to any music.

The girl that was thin and agile couldn't sing worth a darn and couldn't dance. Who was better? Neither.

I went into the garage, asked the girl to look at me and told her about all her wonderful gifts, talents and abilities. I then told her about all her friend's gifts, talents and abilities. I explained how they may not have had the same gifts and talents, but that they could HELP one another in the areas where the other excelled. She could help her friend to sing, dance and ice skate and her friend could support her in trying to stay on the balance beam.

Once they realized they were both special and could both help the other, the fight and upset stopped, and smiles returned to their faces. It was no longer about who was more superior.

Again, we recognize one another's differences and we support each other in our differences. We don't segregate and exclude one another, we embrace our differences. We share our differences to brighten the world with variety and spice!

BRACKETS

Holds the Staffs together -

The TREBLE vs. the BASS CLEFF (Higher vs. Lower)

> i.e.   A gifted higher intellect supporting a
> challenged intellect with a good heart,
> who deserves a chance to succeed in this
> world.

I can relate to this. As I shared earlier, I may have been in honors/academic classes in school, but I didn't have to study hard. I am grateful for the gift of my intellect, but that's just it, it is a gift.

As a result, I was invited to join the Honor Society in High school and Phi Theta Kappa Honor Society at my 2 year college. The thing I loved about the Honor Society was its purpose to give back to the community. In order to stay in the Honor Society, you not only had to keep up your grade point average, but perform a specific number of volunteer service hours in the community.

Besides that, with my personality and enjoyment of writing, I became a charter member of the society and the Public Relations Officer.

Yes, I had some students and teachers make comments that they felt the Honor Society wasn't appropriate because it segregated students.

This is where a group can be seen as good or bad. On the one hand, a group allows a place for like-minded people to be able to talk and relate to one another. It can appear as if the group is shutting out people.

This is something to ponder. Do we just not have any groups? I'd say no, as long as the group doesn't put down those not in the group.

My goal wasn't to set out to teach you how to read music, so I'll stop at this point with the comparisons.

There's a lot more to music, but by now, you've gotten the idea, I hope!

Basically, I wanted to give you something to think about, to allow you to 'see things from a different view', to open discussion about the subject of intolerance and prejudice.

I wanted, as I've done with myself, to allow us to examine our own personal prejudices. To look back at our lives and see where we may have acquired a prejudice without realizing.

I wanted to open a dialogue between faiths, cultures and personality types, to make people comfortable with talking about intolerance and prejudice.

I was talking to my mother about this book, this evening. She said, 'Helen, it needs to be written down for people to see.'

I agree, there is so much good in this world, so many good people. I believe we teach what we need to learn. I'm grateful I've gotten in touch with my unknown/unacknowledged prejudices, and I'm hoping this will help the rest of the world to do the same.

CHAPTER 4

STRUCK A CHORD or A Ha!

Will I never learn? All things in good time! I was frustrated with myself for not having worked on my book in awhile. I was beating myself up over not finishing it.

Well! There I was, driving down a busy road, due to it being December (Holiday season traffic), and what do I see? An angel, sent to give me a message. He was wearing a bright orange turban on his head, and had a full face beard that was at least 5 inches long!

He was running along the side of the road at a busy intersection, with his traveling companion. They were smiling and running quickly towards their car. I can only imagine, why? Possibly the car broke down and they had gone to call someone, who knows?

Anyway, I initially started to smile at the site. Then, I thought, "You know, if this gentleman were among others of his belief, sect, country – he wouldn't be standing out at all", so why should 'I' be thinking about this at all?

Why should I notice his difference? Why should I not be looking past his exterior and noticing his inner soul? Why 'is it' that I'm so focused on his outer appearance. I was actually smiling at the site, because of having been in that same situation, myself. I was recalling having to deal with a vehicle that had broken down along the highway and having to deal with it myself. But then, I started feeling guilty about feeling the empathy of the moment because I was 'recognizing the gentleman's difference in appearance. My awareness of his difference in appearance was taking away from my ability to enjoy the empathy I was feeling for his plight.

Then, AHA, it *STRUCK A CHORD* in me! In that moment, I realized why it has taken me over nine years to get focused and finish this book!

Experiencing, that scenario, along the road, at that particular time is what gave me the insight for the last chapter of this book!

We are MEANT to notice the DIFFERENCES! We are MEANT to acknowledge the DIFFERENCES! The DIFFERENCES are what make the SONG OF LIFE!

Come on! We 'have' to acknowledge our differences! I have a cosmetology license, also. If we don't acknowledge the different skin types, hair types, etc. we wouldn't need to make different products which embrace our differences.

By acknowledging the differences, we can better SERVE one another! The idea is to make life easier or more beautiful for one another! The 'gift is in the giving'.

We need to recognize our differences, and provide service to each other's differences with love, acknowledgement, and acceptance.

Think about it! If we IGNORE the differences, due to FEAR of causing prejudice, we ignore the BEAUTY of life expressing!

If we IGNORED all the DIFFERENT notes and their VALUES on a sheet of music, we wouldn't be able to INTERPRET the music and EXPRESS its beautiful sound.

If we were AFRAID to acknowledge the differences in the expression of sheet music – it would be a monotone.

If we are AFRAID to acknowledge our differences, we don't HONOR our INDIVIDUALITY and what makes us who we are! A huge, beautiful, variety of LIFE EXPRESSING!

I was listing to a news report on the radio the other morning. The newscaster noted that the honeybee population was dwindling. I can't criticize people for fearing and wanting to remove bees from their homes and yards, when they take up residence. I spent 45 years of my life being afraid of bees, spiders and other insects.

Something 'clicked' a few years back and I realized that I could cohabitate with bees and spiders, let them be, respect them, and not need to be fearful. I now have the ultimate respect for insects and the roles they play.

I've gotten to the point where I can be relaxed when a bee is flying near me and actually welcome it, being in awe of its purpose in this world. Once I welcomed bees around me, I was awestruck by an insect known as an 'assassin bug' that I encountered. I had never seen one of these insects in my life; I researched it and found it to be an amazing creature.

Think of the cockroach, we don't want them in our homes, yet they serve a purpose in nature as 'garbage disposal' insects. These amazing insects have been around since pre-historic times. Should we not live in amazement of these creatures?

The reason I bring up insects, having fears and phobias and wanting to 'remove' them from our existence rather than accept them, is that we interfere with the balance of nature and life when not accepting and honoring these different types of life, expressing; such as with the honeybee. Rather than killing a nest full of bees, acknowledging its purpose and service to this world and helping it to continue to exist, to relocate, would be the more respectful option.

Another thought I've had over the years, with respect for life in the plant kingdom. How do you feel about weeds?

I've often noticed, no matter what 'mankind' does to try and stop the expression of life in relation to weeds, nature always wins. For example, we've been paving roads and covering 'the earth' with cement, etc. for years. Yet, what do you notice? Do you see the strength of weeds when they find a way to get through cracked pavement, parking lots, concrete? I find it fascinating, that no matter what we do, the strength of a weed always prevails!

The beauty of this is, no matter what mankind does, life will always continue to express! While we may have domesticated animals, evolved plants into beautiful flowers, edible vegetables, etc.; no matter what we do, if we weren't around, life would go on, expressing as it needed.

For example, look at how, even after a volcano erupts and appears to destroy everything in its path, as time goes by, plants reappear!

Take a look at the destructive landscape of the 1986 Chernobl nuclear reactor disaster. I saw a documentary showing how 'life' has returned to this area, even after mankind appeared to render it lifeless with radiation.

Knowing all of the above, how can we not respect life in all its forms and varieties? No matter whether the life is a plant, animal, or human; we all have a purpose on this earth and we all deserve respect, no matter HOW WE LOOK. What gives us the right to note that a person of one culture, race, background, belief, etc. is better than another?

All life is beautiful; it's all part of the song!

By ACKNOWLEDGING our differences, our unique ways, our unique beliefs … we allow the beautiful music of life to self-express. We allow the 'color' of the music/melody to come through.

Whether we feel a deep, dark pain from the melody, sound and chords or whether we feel bright, upbeat, glad as a result of the sound, it's all good! In fact it's great! The wonderful feeling and expression of the music serves a purpose.

The differences in cultures, religions, organizations, abilities, emotional states and changes in beliefs all make the beautiful sound of life!

We make life a song! And, it's beautiful.

Like music, like flowers, like rainbows, like vegetables, like insects, like animals – we are meant to be different, have different roles, different variations, textures, colors, styles, beliefs, talents, gifts, etc.

We are meant to BE. (This brings to mind a song by Neil Diamond titled 'Be'. It was used in the movie, 'Jonathan Livingston Seagull. It's worth hearing.)

Hear the color of the tone, feel the variations of the beat of life, see the magnificent variations, all the ways life can express itself in different melodies.

Feel, see and hear the creation, movement and expression of life!

Honor it!   Feel it!   See it!

Share it!   Tolerate it!   Respect it!

I see beautiful changes happening in my community, in my State, in my Country in relation to tolerance and acknowledgement of the self-worth of one another.

I want, so much, for this beautiful change to become infectious around the globe! I want so much for this book to be translated into every language of the world, so that past prejudice and intolerance doesn't keep repeating.

It brings to mind the lyrics of a song:

"I'd like to teach the world to sing, in perfect harmony..." by The New Seekers

It also brings to mind another appropriate song:

THERE'S A NEW WORLD COMIN'
(Anita Simone)

There's a new world comin'
And it's just around the bend –
There's a new world comin'
This one's comin' to an end –
There's a new world comin',
One that we've been dreamin' of
Comin' in peace, comin' in joy, comin in love!

MAKE LIFE A SONG

Just can't dance to it?

Take lessons! Take some life lessons!   EDUCATE YOURSELF AND OTHERS…

Quoting the song: Let's 'live life like a song, let's sing it together, let's take our hearts and dip them in rhyme' – and 'hope (know) that it lasts for a long, long time.'

'Turn the beat around'. (*Gloria Estefan and The Miami Sound Machine*)

FEEL that rhythm.

Open your HEART to the pulse of life… to that beat.

DO YOU FEEL IT... that beautiful rhythm of life?

Do you HEAR it, blending?

All the notes, chords, styles, color of tone…

Isn't it beautiful, that melodic, diversity of Life?

Ah, isn't Life is a Song?

About the Author

Helen Marie Szollosy is a woman of many talents and gifts, a jack of all trades, of sorts. Helen was born into a family of 5 children, which later grew into 7! She came from emotionally strong, hard working parents. The dysfunctional challenges of her family only aided in creating a family of loving, compassionate, understanding adults. At the age of 49, she came to realize the beauty of life and its gifts, no matter how they are presented. Helen believes any occurrence in her life is a gift wrapped in disguise.

Helen had many labels placed on her, growing up, which impacted how she approached life. Having been told, early on in life, that she was too quiet, only an average reader and couldn't sing, as well as many other labels, it is now amazing that she is an independent business woman, motivational inspirational speaker, singer (not discovering her singing voice until age 40!) and has done local, volunteer stage acting! She now sees beyond these labels and realizes she can be and achieve anything she wants!

Helen enjoys using her growth from early and current life experiences through her intention to motivate and inspire others to see the beautiful music of life! Her motto is to *Live Life! Laugh Often!* She uses her 'SMILE CAMPAIGN', as seen on her website, www.lafolot.com to make smiles spread across the world!